BLUE HORIZONS

MIKE MCQUEEN
DAVID PATERSON
IAIN ROY

PEAK PUBLISHING

First published in Great Britain by:
Peak Publishing Ltd.,
88 Cavendish Road,
London SW12 0DF.

ISBN 0 9521908 5 0
Cataloguing in British Library publication data applied for.

Blue Horizons
1. Travel
2. Photography

Other titles in series with this volume:
Heart of the Himalaya – Travels in Deepest Nepal (ISBN 0 9521908 2 6)
The Cape Wrath Trail – A 200-Mile Walk Thro' the NW Highlands (ISBN 0 9521908 1 8)
London – City on a River (ISBN 0 9521908 3 4)
A Long Walk on the Isle of Skye (ISBN 0 9521908 4 2)

Front cover photograph: Fiji (M. McQueen)

Designed by Peak Publishing
Typeset in Opus 11/14
Originated & printed by:
C&C Offset Printing Co. Ltd., Hong Kong

CONTENTS

Sunrise, Kauai island, Hawaii

Bay Bridge, San Francisco

The east ridge of Lobuche Peak, Nepal Himalaya

PREFACE

THIS BOOK COULD BE SEEN as the ultimate whistle-stop tour – around the world in 144 pages – with Europe reduced to a chapter and all the southern hemisphere dismissed in even less. But that is not how I hope you will see it. Three good friends, all photographers, have tried to distill their work down to its essence and to convey some of the excitement to be found, out in the world, searching for images.

We came to photography by different routes, but at much the same time in the early and mid-1960s. Iain Roy and I met when we were both students in Edinburgh, and he took instinctively to photography as a part of his fine-art studies. His work is, and always has been that of an artist whose chosen medium is photography. I ran across Mike McQueen in the early '70s when we were both fledgling professionals, trying to make a living in the embryonic Scottish advertising scene. He had studied at photographic college and already had experience as a photojournalist, whereas I had no formal training and had learned what little I knew of photography by poring over the works of the acknowledged masters – Ansel Adams, Eugene Smith, Ernst Haas, Henri Cartier Bresson, Man Ray, Edward Weston, Bill Brandt, Paul Strand, Walker Evans – the list even then was almost endless, as I discovered.

We would never dare to claim any sort of place with the greats who were my original inspiration but perhaps we share part of their motivation. The world is never less than fascinating; sometimes horrifying, often beautiful; but much of what we love is changing, vanishing. Through the simple act of recording an image – a vanishing tribe, a dying species or simply a fleeting moment of beauty – photography can help to ensure that *something* is preserved. But there is more to it than that. With war, poverty and pollution daily in our newspapers and on our screens, it can be easy to despair, and easier still to lose sight of how glorious much of our world still is. Photography is often used to show us the darker side (and rightly so), but it can also say, "Now – look at THIS! "

There is, for all photographers, the challenge of trying to construct intuitive and original images, and great joy when we occasionally succeed. If the Victorian era had its golden age, the last few decades of the 20th century have seen a new and more democratic age of travel. Vast numbers of people nowadays (in the west at least) have the opportunity to visit not only tourist attractions but the furthest corners of the seven continents. There is nowhere on the planet which has not been photographed many times, both by tourists, artists and professionals. How then, can we achieve any kind of originality or freshness of vision? I'm not sure I know, but *trying harder* is probably part of the answer. Spending long periods getting to know one's chosen territory is a real advantage; having the time to move slowly, ideally on foot, through great tracts of arctic Greenland, the Himalayas or even the more intimate spaces of Europe is an experience not everyone can share. In showing these images we acknowledge the many privileges we have enjoyed.

Over the years there have been many collaborations among the three authors, including Himalayan expeditions; this book is only the latest venture. Mike and I had been planning it together for a while, deciding rather late in the day to invite Iain to contribute some of his unique work from Greenland. Both these and his thoughtful Himalayan images make a crucial contribution to the final result. What amazing good fortune we have had; how fantastic the journey has been, so far.   *David Paterson, London. March '99.*

WESTERN EUROPE

BY CONVENTION, MAP-MAKERS place Europe at the centre of the world, and this is still where many Europeans believe they belong. Considering the continent's influence throughout history, the claim may seem justified. It was from European ports, after all, that the legendary explorers 'discovered' other lands – according to this perspective. Moreover, the classical architecture of Greece and Rome, the evolution of democracy, the flowering of Renaissance art, the philosophy of the Enlightenment and the power of Industrial Revolution and Empire have all exported institutions which can be hard to see beyond. Yet if this Eurocentricity was once a strength, it may also be a cultural Achilles' heel. For we have been slow to recognise there are other traditions besides our own and, though there is much to be proud of in past achievements, we have still to outgrow the feudal weakness of not living easily with our neighbours.

Most Europeans, whether they care to admit it or not, are themselves the product of cultural fusion. Between the Eurals and the Atlantic a complex mix of peoples has settled. Since the great migrations of the Celts in the Iron Age and the epic wanderings of the 'Barbarian' tribes across the later Roman Empire, the origins of Europe's peoples have often been distant from their eventual 'homelands'. The Norman knights who followed William the Conqueror to England were, for instance, the direct descendants of pagan Norse raiders, and their cousins, who ruled twelfth century Sicily, held court in quasi-oriental grandeur. In fact, at several pivotal times, Europe's scholars, musicians and artists were to draw upon sources far beyond their own frontiers.

Believing, perhaps, in Francis Bacon's maxim that travel is the best education, the authors of this volume seized every opportunity to see for themselves how one's own cultural identity is not diminished but enriched by appreciating what other people and places can offer. We saw no inconsistency in thinking of ourselves as *Europeans* who happened to be Scottish, perhaps unconsciously invoking those ancient bonds between the northern Celts and our kindred Gaels in a manner not always shared by our southern neighbours.

The world has moved on since the carefree age of the 1960s, and Europe's place within the global village may have been in some ways diminished. Then, only the most intrepid travellers struck out farther than the Bosphorus and packaged holidays were mostly confined to familiar locations. Now, world travel on a scale hitherto unimaginable has come within reach of the many, and each day the insatiable monster of intercontinental tourism threatens to destroy the very objects of its desires. Has that unique sense of *genius loci* one used to feel in front of the great monuments - the Acropolis, Chartres Cathedral, or the north wall of the Eiger - been lost in the process? Those who still journey to such places would surely hope not, but their search for a truly solitary experience may turn out to be a very long one.

East or west, these days one is never far from the fast food diner, and jeans and trainers are the new lingua franca. Even so, if travelling to Istanbul on the Orient Express, exploring the alleyways of Lisbon, or looking out across the frozen Neva from the galleries of the Hermitage may no longer be quite the novelty they were, Europe's past cannot be obliterated so easily; history is etched deeply into every square metre of her cities, villages, and mountains. This is the kind of beauty which accretes over centuries, though it may require some knowledge to be fully appreciated. Perhaps it is that perennial fascination with the historic which still attracts millions from around the globe. Today, they may be disgorged from jumbo-jets with back-pack and 'Rough Guide', or tour in camper-vans – a far cry from the style of characters from the pages of Henry James or F. Scott Fitzgerald. Yet still they come, drawn back to what many still intuitively regard as the origin of much that is good and true in the world.   *I. Roy*

Paris and the Eiffel Tower by night

La Grande Arche, La Défense, Paris

The Eiffel Tower (right)

Europe's greatest monument – the Alps – swings through Austria, Switzerland, France and northern Italy in a dazzling array of peaks hundreds of miles long. The relatively northern latitude means that these mountains, only rarely rising above 4000 metres (less than half the height of Mount Everest), are thickly snow-covered at all seasons and heavily glaciated.

Here the top section of the Bossons Glacier, with a fresh covering of autumn snow, is still in early morning shadow as it begins its fall from high on the upper slopes of Mont Blanc towards the Chamonix Valley, some two thousand metres below. The rounded summit of Mont Blanc (4807m) is just visible to the right of the brightly-lit plume of snow.

The hills of southern Spain – the Serrania de Ronda

Ludwigsburg Palace, Bavaria

Schwäbischall, Bavaria (right)

The port of Algeciras, southern Spain

Fishermen haul nets off Malaga, southern Spain

High plains near Toledo, central Spain

The courtyard of the Great Mosque, Cordoba

The Great Mosque, Cordoba

Il Duomo, Florence (right)

Piazza dei Cavalieri, Pisa

Lucca, Tuscany

Palermo, Sicily

St Petersburg – Leningrad when this photograph was taken

NORTH EAST GREENLAND

Melting sea-ice in Hurry Inlet, Kap Stewart

Throughout the 1990s Iain Roy has been photographing the fjord region of north east Greenland in a series of summer expeditions. He is a member of a group of Arctic enthusiasts whose varied activities also include making botanical studies and mapping unknown Inuit sites. Recently, UK media have reported NASA studies which show how the Greenland ice-cap is melting at a rate which could precipitate climate changes across the north Atlantic by 'switching off' the Gulf Stream.

GEOPHYSICAL CONDITIONS IN GREENLAND would, at first, seem to have little in common with our temperate British seasons. Greenland is synonymous with polar ice and snow; a place of mighty mountains and glaciers. It is indeed a land of extremes, with four fifths of its surface buried under a huge mantle of ice up to ten thousand feet (3000m.) thick. In the lands of the Arctic, summers are brief affairs and the winters long, cold, and hard. Yet we should remember that Cape Farewell, at the southernmost tip of the Greenland ice-cap, actually shares its latitude with St. Petersburg – and the Shetland Islands. It is only because of the warm Atlantic currents, the celebrated Gulf Stream, that the British Isles enjoy such a mild, if wettish, climate.

Greenland was once part of the same land mass as Britain. Over many eons, mid-Atlantic volcanic pressures have driven the rocks of east Greenland and the 'Ancient Foreland' of the north west Highlands an ocean apart until the huge island, first dubbed Greenland by the Norse outlaw Eirik the Red a mere thousand years ago, became a remote and isolated place. Despite its connections from the time of the Norse settlement or its later re-colonisation by missionaries, whalers and trappers, Greenland is not really thought of as a part of Europe nor of the Americas. It remained a place on the margins of the known world for many centuries, retaining an aura of myth and mystery; a little-known part of the Arctic where the polar climate reaches far south into the Atlantic, a place where icebergs are born. Nevertheless, this mysterious ice-capped island is once again being closely linked to the fate of the British Isles, if only because of the consequences of global warming which, paradoxically, could bring colder and even wetter weather to the northern shores of Britain.

If the melting of the Greenland ice-cap were to accelerate, even by a little, sea levels the world over would rise appreciably. Not only would estuarine and other low-lying areas around England's south and east coasts be at the mercy of rising tide-lines, we are being warned, but also and more significantly, the pan-oceanic currents of warm and cold waters would be drastically re-aligned. Consequently the deeper colder waters off east Greenland would not be held in check; icebergs would no longer come to some natural terminus in the fogs off Newfoundland and a flotsam of ice could well start to spread out across the entire north Atlantic. The prospect of icebergs reaching as far as the northern islands and sea-lochs of Scotland might be no mere science fantasy, and the time-scale over which such consequences might occur could be much more compressed than we would care to imagine, once the geophysical conditions needed to trigger them had reached a critical point. The effect of climatic change on human settlements is, of course, by no means a new phenomenon. Examination of the bio-chemical record imprisoned within the layers of glacial strata, or of the volcanic dust and organic remains embedded in layers of peat, can demonstrate how far-reaching environmental change has occurred in the past. Some such shifts are a matter of historical record – the Romans enjoyed sunnier summers and introduced viticulture to Britain, and traditional Christmas cards reflect images of skaters on frozen ponds and rivers based on a collective memory of 17th century pictorial scenes.

Along the north-east coast of Greenland there lies a labyrinthine system of fjords and sounds, a hidden world locked behind a constantly shifting white off-shore mosaic. Here there was once a native culture. Unusually, considering the insatiable appetite of 19th century Europeans for the unknown and the exotic, little was ever found out about these folk who were only glimpsed once. It was a brief encounter, indeed, when Captain Douglas Clavering, commander of HMS Griper, on an exploratory boat trip into Gael Hamke's Bay, came across a small party of Inuit. He saw their tents of skins and examined bone-tipped harpoons and other artefacts, but on only the second day after their meeting, his ethnographic investigations were cut short. After a demonstration of firearms the natives understandably took fright, and neither they nor their descendants were ever seen again. A German expedition of 1870 which actually searched for the 'eskimo' of the north-east coast found no trace of them, despite having passed close by the site of the largest Inuit village in the region.

Like all branches of Inuit culture, the survival of these tribes must have hung on the most slender of ecological threads. Having learned how to live in one of the most hostile environments on the planet, one could guess their demise was related to changes in the climate – and closely linked to the fate of the species on which they relied. It may be significant that a sub-species of caribou formerly endemic to the north east of Greenland also went into rapid decline during the second half of the 19th century. Research has suggested that a series of partial thaws in successive winters caused the icing up of the lichen which was the animals' staple diet and the herds died out of starvation within a remarkably short period. We know that similar catastrophes have affected caribou populations elsewhere in more recent times. What is significant is the alarming speed with which the caribou, and possibly the Inuit before them, declined to the point of extinction once the environmental scales tipped against them.

All that now remains of the Inuit who lived and hunted in the fjord region are the stone shells of their winter and summer houses, their tent rings, foxtraps, hearths, graves and fragments of drilled bone. Most objects of any serious ethnographic interest, and sadly most of the graves, were pillaged in the 1930s, either by hunters seeking saleable souvenirs or by the first archaeologists to excavate the sites. There is no more poignant emblem of these lost people of the north than a number of curious 'mosaics' – small stone configurations carefully laid out on gravel benches, often in magnificent settings. These are thought to have been the playthings of the children of the villages, representing in miniature their families' dwellings. The fate of these last few souls faced with inexorable decline is hard for us to imagine. Cocooned in our sanitised environments we are distanced, literally and metaphorically, from both the sources of our food and the crucial changes in the eco-system which could well be determining our fate too. These silent stone relics of the lost culture of north east Greenland can speak oceans to those who are prepared to listen.

I. Roy

Sandstone boulder, Milne Land

The cliffs of Bastionen, Ella Island, Narhvalsund

Towards Renland from The Bear Islands

Looking towards Gåseland from Fønbugt

Trappers' hut near the head of Franz Josef Fjord

Midnight sun, Scoresby Sund

Near Bastian Bay, Kühn Island

Sulugssut, Bear Islands

Stranded bergs, east Milne Land

THE MIDDLE EAST

IN THE WEST WE ARE ALL A LITTLE AFRAID of the countries of the Middle East, especially these days when the spectre of (so-called) Islamic extremism looms regularly from our TV screens and newspapers. That the threat, even to innocent visitors, is not an idle one is apparent from events during the late 1990s in Egypt and Yemen. Yet the visitor to most Arab countries, if he or she can penetrate the barriers (which have been erected by a certain amount of mutual ignorance) and the intense reserve of most of the people, will find nothing but the greatest generosity and warmth. At the same time there is a certain lack of privacy for the visitor which is unsettling to Europeans. An unrestrained curiosity on the part of strangers of all ages but especially young children has to be met with the greatest tolerance and patience, since any display of irritation or anger is counter-productive, to say the least. Even after decades of tourism (or perhaps because of it; the behaviour and appearance of many tourists is often fairly bizarre) a Westerner setting foot off the beaten track almost anywhere in North Africa, around the eastern Medi-terranean or in the Gulf states is still quite likely to be treated somewhat like a visitor from outer space.

For the photographer this is all frustrating enough, but in addition there is often a sneaking suspicion that simply by taking photographs at all one is not only offending someone's deepest religious beliefs but probably breaking a number of obscure laws as well. Retribution, in the shape either of a stone-throwing mob or a couple of large policeman, is probably already on its way. Neither of these scenarios is totally far-fetched – it is certainly possible to be stoned in parts of North Africa, or arrested in Saudi Arabia, just for being in a public place with a camera – even if the chance of it happening is probably not very great, and reducing all the time. Around anything which could be considered a tourist attraction, of course, cameras are commonplace. Far from trying to prevent photography, the streetwise kids and locals are much more likely to encourage it, coming up with all sorts of inventive reasons for extracting money in return.

These minor irritations, which in any case can be turned into a source of amusement by the right attitude, are as nothing compared to the many fascinations of these countries, their rich and ancient culture, the glorious architecture of their mosques and palaces, and for the Western traveller the very clear and obvious sense of being somewhere *different*. Then there is the bustling and colourful life of the streets and souks, the vast landscapes, the empty and beautiful deserts and the great wealth of archaelogical remains. All the world knows of the pyramids and Egypt's other fabulous ruins, but Tunisia, Libya, Turkey, Syria, and Jordan are rich with remains from pre-Roman times to the Crusades. Many of these are unheralded even by roadside signs and often completely un-tended, which may not aid their conservation, but does wonders for their atmosphere. It can come as a shock, in such a famous and much-visited location as Petra, to discover that over large areas of the site one is walking on a virtual carpet of Nabatean (pre-Christian) pottery shards.

Mike McQueen once lived for the greater part of a year in Tunisia, and has visited Morocco and Egypt more than once. I have travelled briefly in several of these countries – Morocco, Turkey, Jordan, Saudi Arabia, Oman and the Gulf Emirates, and also Israel (which is different from the others in many ways, but more alike than Israelis might wish) – and still have a yearning for the old Islamic world, in particular the great deserts of Arabia, which one day I hope to satisfy. The 'new' Islamic world of Malaysia and Indonesia is something else, not easy to reconcile with one's notions of what traditional Islam and the languid tropics are all about. The world is full of change –nowhere more than in these very countries – and our concepts of them must change too.

D. Paterson

Statue of Ramses II, Luxor

Pyramid of Cheops, Giza

Statues of Ramses II, Luxor

The Dome of the Rock, Jerusalem

Sunset in the Negev desert, Israel (right)

The Street of Facades, Petra, Jordan

Bedouin Arabs and their horses, Petra

Cappodocia, Turkey

The mountains of Wadi Rum, Jordan (right)

(Clockwise from top left) Tunis; Rabat (Morocco); Luxor; Hurghada (Egypt)

(From top left, clockwise) Fez (Morocco); Oman; Beyshir, & nr. Konya (Turkey)

House entrance, Marrakesh, Morocco

Draa River valley, southern Morocco

Arched gateway, Tangiers

Dunes, Abu Dhabi (right)

HIMALAYAN STATES

THE GREATER HIMALAYA STRETCHES in a sublime arc some fifteen hundred miles (2400 kms), from northern Afghanistan to the borders of Burma at the other end of the subcontinent, and the hill-states which nestle among its foothills have always been something of a byeword for turbulence. Both Tibet and Nepal were closed virtually to all comers until some years after the Second World War, while the northern territories of Pakistan and India were even later in opening their doors and some are still not fully open now. It is the good fortune of modern travellers and mountaineers, however, that many of these restrictions have been gradually easing, and that most of this fascinating region can be visited quite freely.

The sub-continent has long been an area of special interest for the British, though our imperial past may not always have been as glorious as it has been painted. But ever since the days when the British East India Company ran India as its private estate, there has been a strong relationship between the two countries which shows few signs of diminishing, in spite of the inevitable handful of malcontents on both sides. Whereas the East India Company may have only been interested in business and profit, many other influences of Indian culture soon came to bear on the British in India, and there was a considerable amount of cross-fertilisation in the fields of art, literature and architecture.

With the demise of British imperial power in India the relationship changed, but can hardly be said to be less strong than before. Partly due to the expulsions from Uganda in the 1960s, the UK has become home to many tens of thousands who originated in the sub-continent and their descendants, who are an integral part of Britain's multi-cultural society. At the same time, India has become a destination of choice not only for executives seeking contracts, but for a multitude of tourists and travellers, trekkers and mountaineers who contain within their ranks new generations of writers and artists.

Many of these head, of course, straight for the Himalayas.

In the days before Nepal opened her doors to trekkers as well as officially-recognised climbing expeditions, northern Pakistan and India, and especially Kashmir, were strongly favoured and many an 'old-timer' will speak mistily of Kulu and Manali, Lahul and Spiti – regions effectively closed today because of unrest in Kashmir. Baltistan, Ladakh and Zanskar were also known and loved by the cognoscenti, but with the coming of the age of mass travel it was Nepal which suddenly became the place where everyone wanted to go. With its superb mountain scenery, comfortable climate and hospitable people its success seemed unstoppable, and for twenty years or more it was top of many people's lists. Now, the adventure tourists and trekkers are beginning to leak away to the Hindu Kush and the Karakorams, and Kathmandu is no longer the unknown, fabulous Himalayan capital. Perhaps a few too many trekkers queue along the popular routes to Everest and Annapurna, and Nepal is showing signs of becoming a victim of her own success. But those wonderful mountains are still there and will draw climbers and trekkers for as long as Nepal is prepared to welcome them.

Mike McQueen was one of the first Europeans to enter Ladakh when it was re-opened in August 1975, and has also visited Kashmir – in the days when you did not risk your life simply by being there. All three of us have been more than once to Nepal (I have been a frequent visitor, and have made it something of a second home) and are likely to go back, given the opportunity. Perhaps not everyone feels it, these days, but there is still something very special about Nepal, something more than just her unrivalled concentration of high mountains. I believe it has a lot to do with the Buddhist qualities of gentleness and tolerance which are still characteristic of the people of the hills, and if those are ever lost the magic, too, will have gone.

D. Paterson

Porters at Lhonak, below Wedge Peak, Kangchenjunga Himal

Street scene, Srinagar, Kashmir

Floating market, Dal Lake, Kashmir

'Mani' stone, Kali Gandaki valley, Nepal

Peak 6, Makalu Himal, Nepal (right)

Nepal Peak, Kangchenjunga Himal

Landslip near the Ladakh/Kashmir border

Landscape near Kargil, Kashm

Tamur valley near Mitlung, east Nepal

(Left) Rice-fields at Sinam, east Nepal

Woman and child, Ley, Ladakh

(Top) Monks, Ley, Ladakh   Children in Dras, Kashmir

Prayer-flag at Paldol Pass, Ganesh Himal, Nepal

In the Ghunsa Valley, east Nepal (right)

78

THE KALI GANDAKI VALLEY cuts north-south through western Nepal, penetrating the main Himalayan chain, and has for centuries been a main conduit for trade and culture between the Indian subcontinent, south of the Himalayas, and Tibet and the rest of central Asia to the north. In the autumn of 1996 Iain Roy and I spent a month in the Kali Gandaki region.

The central section of the valley is flanked by Annapurna to the west and Dhaulagiri, another 8000m. giant, to the east; on the Annapurna side a high parallel ridge separates the valley from the main mountain mass. We had determined to spend a few days, away from the busy trekking trail down in the valley, up on this high ridge known as Thulobugin. Paths were hard to find; the flanks of the ridge were steep and rose relentlessly to a height of some 4250m. from the banks of the Kali Gandaki river at 2000m. At last, enquiring in local villages and from passing herders, we found a way.

On the first night, halfway up to the ridge, we camped near the crude shelter of a solitary cowherd, his beasts wandering the pine- and bamboo-thickets which dotted the vast slopes. Nearby, a level patch of ground was the site of a number of small stone tables whose meaning we could not even guess at. A flat slab would be poised, level, on the top of a supporting boulder or small cairn; there were perhaps twenty such monuments dotted around a small area. We looked and pon-

Monastic cell? on the Thulobugin Ridge below Nilgiri South.

dered for a while, but the next morning continued our climb up towards the main ridge, the enigma of the stones forgotten for the time being.

Thulobugin Ridge is truly a spectacular place, a narrow, swooping ridge strung between a series of minor summits, with Annapurna and Dhaulagiri seemingly just a stone's-throw away on either hand, in the crystal air. Past inhabitants of the region had obviously felt its power also, as we soon discovered. Where we finally stepped on to the crest of the main ridge an inscribed stone slab announced that this was a hallowed area, and that no meat must be eaten. Soon other groups of small stone altars and larger monuments of various kinds began to appear. Some were truly altar-shaped; as we progressed along the ridge the most common remains could be interpreted as a kind of monastic cell. Clearly built to a pattern – gabled walls, which had probably once supported a wattle roof, enclosed a hearth and flagstoned floor. The interior of the taller gable was often adorned with a niche.

They remain as a puzzling addition to the list of stone monuments with which Buddhist highlanders have decorated their landscape – stupas, chortens, prayer-walls and 'mani-stones' are found near most villages, every monastery and in any locality regarded as sacred. But no-one could (or would) tell us the hidden meaning of the Stones of Thulobugin.

Buddhist chorten above Kagbeni, Mustang

The summit-cone of Dhaulagiri, west Nepal

Barley dries near Kagbeni, west Nepal (right)

Chorten above Muktinath, Mustang

ASPECTS OF ASIA

YOU COULD SPEND A LIFETIME travelling the continent of Asia and not see more than a tiny fraction of it. Look at a map of the world and marvel at Asia's vastness compared with tiny Europe stuck on its western end. Study a map of population-density and marvel even more at the emptiness of most of this huge land-mass. Immense regions of Siberia, Mongolia, Turkestan, Tibet and northern China have an average of less than two human beings per square kilometer, and together with those areas – still almost empty of humanity – which have up to five people per km^2 the entire central region of the continent is included. (By comparison, the UK has a pop-ulation density of around 250.) 19th-century explorers wrote of travelling for weeks in areas such as northern Tibet without seeing another human being. Little has changed today.

The reason for this is straightforward, and can readily be understood from the air. Fly over any part of central Iran, Afghanistan, northern Pakistan or India, Tibet, Mongolia or Siberia and you wonder not why there are so few inhabitants down there but how anyone can survive at all, so barren and inhospitable does the terrain appear. A brown, sere wilder-ness disappears over the horizon in every direction, relieved only by the occasional glint of ice-clad mountains, barely changing hour upon hour as your flight proceeds.

What might be called the coastal fringe of this giant conti-nent, on the other hand, is densely populated. All of southern India, southern and eastern China, IndoChina, Taiwan, Korea and Japan make up in population what the steppes of central Asia lack. Interestingly, except for much of India and China, these countries are themselves extremely mountainous, so that their habitable territory is limited to coastal strips and major river-valleys. As a result their populations are extremely concentrated and have often adapted to limits on personal space and privacy which Europeans or Americans would find hard to accept. It comes as something of a shock to enter a

typical home in Tokyo or Osaka for the first time, to find per-haps three generations of a relatively affluent family living in a space little larger than many a western middle-class kitchen/dining-room; or to visit the teeming apartment-blocks of Singapore, Hong Kong or Shanghai where living-space is even less generous than in Japan, and life (and noise) goes on ceaselessly, 24 hours a day. We in the west are spoiled and would find it very hard to live, long-term, in conditions which millions must tolerate, but the cities of Asia have their own special fascination for the traveller. As photographers our instincts are for the wide-open spaces and what little wilder-ness is left on our rapidly-shrinking planet, but when in the east somehow it is the cities which have drawn us in. While the mind recoils from some of their aspects – the noise, the apparent chaos and (to our eyes) the terrible over-crowding – it is these qualities which give the cities the vigour and vivacity which are ultimately so attractive.

To be able to survive there, some rapid adjustments have to be made. I once lived for six months in Tokyo and had two very hard months once the novelty had worn off and the con-stant crowds had begun to unsettle me. Luckily I was able to adapt and enjoy the rest of my time there, but many pre-con-ceptions had to be jettisoned and perhaps that is the key. Some years later, in India, I found myself chafing again at the throngs of untidy humanity which 'spoiled' the views of the wonderful Mogul architecture I wanted to see and photo-graph. On a third visit to the Taj Mahal, this time at the crack of dawn 'to avoid the crowds', I had to laugh at myself and my naiveté as I joined the queue of many patient Indian visi-tors and pilgrims who were already waiting to be admitted to what is one of their most revered shrines. The Indian Tourist Board image of the deserted Taj floating above the perfect mirror of an ornamental pond would have to wait for another time; or perhaps another life.

D. Paterson

Village shrine, Gumma prefecture, N. Japan

Climbers on the summit of Mt. Kita, Japanese Alps

Pressure-vessel at Kofu, central Japan

Asakusa Kannon Temple, Tokyo

Musicians at the Asakusa Kannon Festival, Tokyo

Bullet train, Tokyo Station

Mount Fuji

Wanchai, downtown Hong Kong, by night

Tiananmen Gate, Beijing (right)

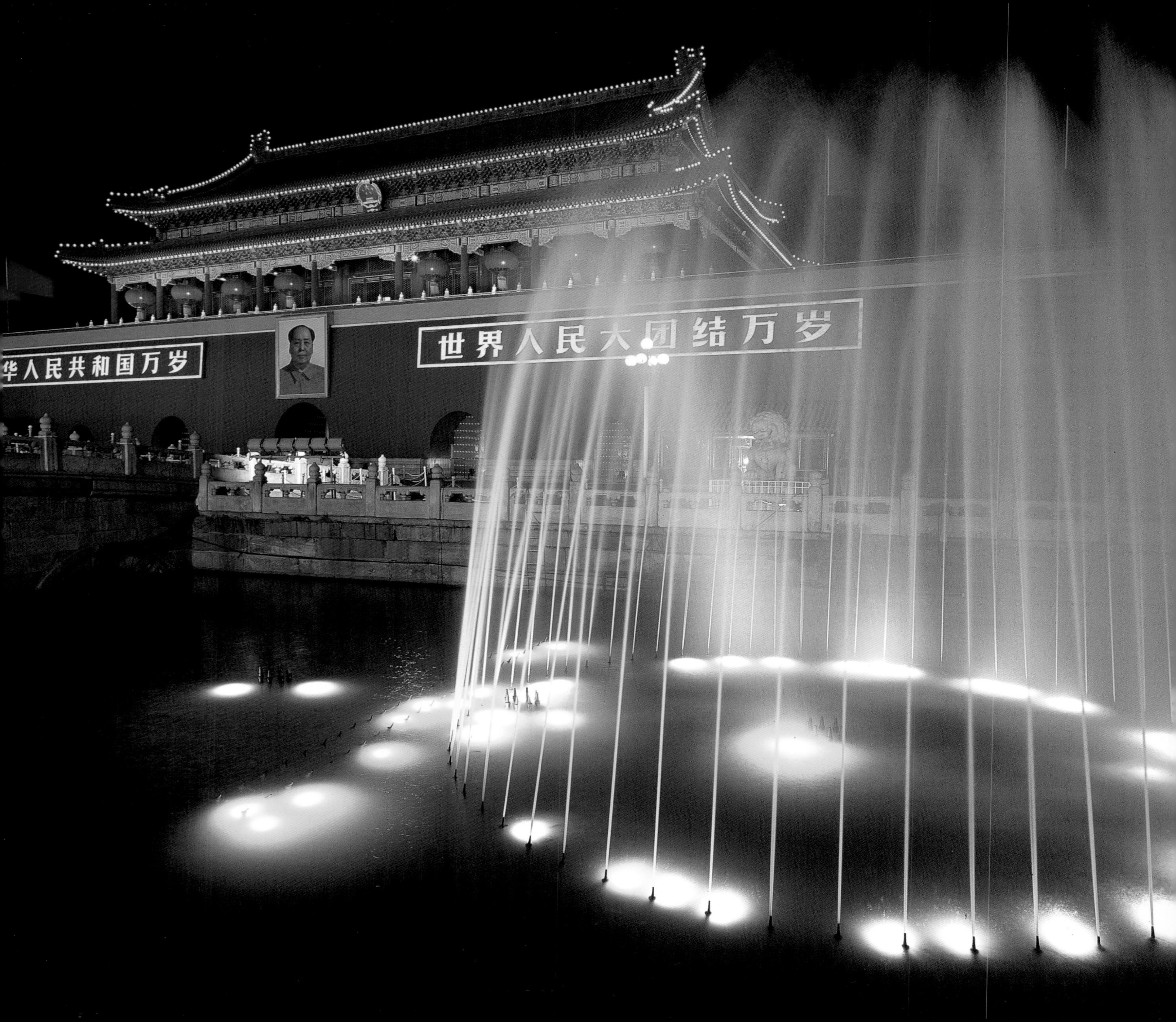
华人民共和国万岁
世界人民大团结万岁

The wall of the Forbidden City, Beijing

Bicycles outside the Forbidden City

Shop in Panaji, Goa

The Red Flag, Tiananmen Square, Beijing

The Taj Mahal, Agra

The Palace of the Winds, Jaipur (right)

Country road near Jaipur

Coconut palms, Vagatar, Goa

Christian shrine and sacred cow, Chapora, Goa

Fruit-seller, Colva beach, Goa

SOUTHERN LATITUDES

EN ROUTE BY AIR FROM SYDNEY to Hawaii all that can be seen from the 'plane window is the deep blue of the Pacific some 30,000 feet below. Hour after hour after hour the surface of the boundless ocean, etched only by the minute "v" of an occasional ship's wake, was unrelieved by any sight of land. It is something I will never forget.

The facts and figures about the Pacific Ocean are quite astounding. Its area of around 165 million square kms is large enough to swallow up the entire land mass of the planet and still leave an ocean more than one and a half times the size of the United States of America. Contained in this vastness is a population of a mere seven million people – fewer than that of Greater London – living on islands which are sprinkled like grains of rice on the surface of an enormous lake. Physically these islands vary from being little more than a sand-bar barely visible at high tide, through countless coral islands fringed by archetypal sugar-white beaches around electric-blue lagoons, to the larger tropical, and actively volcanic, islands such as Big Island, Hawaii, with its twin peaks of over 4000m.

During more than ten centuries of seafaring, Polynesians set sail from Samoa heading for the Marquesas Islands to the east and onwards from there to all parts of the Pacific – from New Zealand in the south to the most northerly inhabited archipelago of Hawaii. All of this was achieved without the aid of compass or charts. Using only their knowledge of currents, winds, stars and the flights of birds, with their double-hulled canoes laden with breadfruit, sweet potatoes, fowls, pigs, and dogs bred for food, they embarked to colonise the islands.

These jewel-like islands and atolls have been magnets for many decades to travellers and tourists seeking to escape from the pressures and stresses encountered in their everyday lives, and as a result most of the Pacific Islands count tourism as their number one industry. Inevitably the pressures of tourism are putting a strain on the islands and islanders alike, and uncontrolled expansion of the industry could seriously affect not only conditions for the islanders themselves but the nature of the experience that the visitor expects in these tropical paradises. This can be a difficult quality to identify precisely, but it may have something to do with a tranquillity created by the special beauty of the place combined with the usually balmy weather. This tranquillity is best reflected in the gentle nature of the true native people of the Pacific Islands.

A source of some tension in the area has been caused by the degree to which the native peoples of the region have been subsumed by more aggressively enterprising incomers. On Fiji, for instance, native Fijians and the descendants of Indian indentured labourers, who began arriving in the country in 1878, have a roughly equal proportion of the 800,000 population. As a consequence of stresses created by the very different approaches to life of the two communities, two (bloodless) military coups occurred in 1987. It was several years before visitors felt that it was safe to return, and even now Fiji's tourist industry has yet to reach its pre-1987 levels.

In stark contrast to the classic image one has of the Fiji islands there is Hawaii. This small chain of eight inhabited volcanic islands – the 51st state of America – whose indigenous population is only 18% of the one million total, bridges the gap between the Pacific idyll and the go-getting energy of the USA. The latter is mostly found on the island of Oahu where most of Hawaii's population live, and where famous locations such as Waikiki Beach exert their pull on the seven million visitors who arrive annually. My preference for photographing wild and dramatic landscapes took me first to the island of Kauai with its breathtaking Napali Coast and Waimea Canyon and from there to Big Island, famous for its dramatic volcanic peaks and the red lava flow which plunges into the ocean at Kalapana, creating a huge plume of steam and adding a few more meters daily to the still evolving island.   *M.McQueen.*

Sunrise, Sydney Harbour Bridge

Sydney Opera House

Sydney Harbour (right)

Napali coast, Kuaui, Hawaii

Waimea Canyon, Kuaui

Fishermen on Malololailai, Fiji

Sanur beach, Bali

Rice terraces near Ubud, Bali

Malolo, Fiji (not to be confused with Malololailai!)

Sanur, Bali (right)

Malololailai, Fiji

WESTERN USA

THE UNITED STATES OF AMERICA is the one country which everyone knows, or thinks they do. We are so bombarded by images of the fifty-one states on TV, in the cinema and in the press, that the whole *enchilada* from New York to San Francisco seems as familiar as home (whether home is Inverness, Paris, Cape Town or Tokyo). The USA is not just another country, however, it is a sub-continent four thousand kilometers east-west by two thousand north-south (ignoring the further-flung states of Hawaii and Alaska), and for every monument or landmark which we know from films and photographs there are a dozen more which are equally worthwhile but totally unknown. There is hardly a state which does not harbour some natural wonder, or several, and this is before we include man-made phenomena of which the Golden Gate Bridge and the Manhattan skyline are just two out of many.

UK visitors to the States tend to concentrate on some fairly limited aspects, and this is understandable. Confronted with this giant land-mass and a bewildering number of states and cities (most, when the truth is told, completely unfamiliar to the average European) many people opt for children-friendly Florida and its warm climate, the excitement of New York and San Francisco, or the winter sports of Aspen or Denver. But of course there is lots, lots more. I had worked a few times on the eastern sea-board on industrial assignments for commercial clients, but had never ventured further afield. Somewhat daunted by the vastness of the place, I avoided the issue by telling myself I would never try to photograph the United States until I could devote at least six months to the project; which meant, effectively, that I never would.

In the spring of 1995 Mike McQueen suggested that we should consider sharing expenses on a trip through some of the western states, and came round one day to show me his collection of maps, references and notes, and to explain what he thought we could achieve in a good deal less than six months over there. I was instantly hooked, and in the autumn of that year the trip was to become a reality.

Yosemite, the Rockies, Yellowstone, the Grand Canyon – we have all heard those names and think we understand what they represent – but who knows anything of Bryce Canyon, Zion, Cedar Breaks or Mesa Verde? I did not, but I was about to have my eyes opened. The western states contain many stunning landscapes, any one of which would be famous if it were situated in Europe but which are obscured among the abundance of similar features which the United States can offer. There were days when almost every turn in the road revealed some magnificent but unexpected sight, and if the drama of mountains and canyons became too much there were long calm days, driving slowly through the empty plains of Utah and Arizona, and the deserts of California or Nevada. Autumn days were cool on the heights of Yosemite and Mesa Verde – new snow in the San Juan Mountains – warm in the Mohave Desert, hot down in Death Valley then cold again up among the giant trees of Sequoia National Park.

Change of every kind rushed by. The one constant seemed to be the emptiness of these landscapes, and for much of the time we were travelling through areas given over either to military or Indian reservations. Both groups hid themselves and their settlements well away from public roads, and for many hours each day the only evidence of a human presence, as we drove, might be an occasional shack or a distant herd of cattle – these arid lands with their scorching summer climate can support very little (which is why they were given to the Indians). On a day's drive one might see just one small township; famous Route 66 was a study in abandonment, its crazed tarmac lurching through dusty ghost-towns, and the Mohave an empty wilderness of cactus and rattling sage-brush. I never expected to come back from the US homesick for Marlboro' County, but four years later I still am.

D. Paterson

Dusk over Zion Canyon, Utah

The valley floor, Yosemite

El Capitan, Yosemite

Railroad crossing near Cow Springs, Arizona

Pickup truck in Flagstaff, Arizona (right)

Giant Sequoia, Sequoia National Park

Cedar and aspen woods, Cedar Breaks, Utah

Northern Arizona, near Kayenta

Zion Canyon National Park, Utah

'Hoodoo' erosion pinnacle, Bryce Canyon

Bryce Canyon, Utah (right)

136

Aspen grove, Cedar Breaks, Utah

Looking vertically upwards in Antelope Canyon, a 'slot canyon', near Page, Arizona. Slot canyons are landscape features unique to this part of the United States – very deep, very narrow gullies formed when vast quantities of trapped floodwater poured out through fissures in soft sandstone, sculpting them in a matter of a few days to the beautiful and abstract shapes seen today.

(Both pages) Dunes at Mesquite Flats, Death Valley, California

The Grand Canyon

The "Mitten" Buttes, Monument Valley (right)

Mike McQueen was born in Monifeith, near Dundee, and educated in Leicester where he studied photography after a short period working in industry. He worked briefly as a photojournalist in Leicester before moving back to Scotland where he freelanced for advertising and design agencies as well as the housing-action charity, Shelter. He has been based in London since 1980 and is a member of the photo-agency Impact. His photographs have appeared in many leading publications, and he worked for some time for The Observer. He now works as a landscape and travel photographer selling his work through a leading international photolibrary, and this has taken him around the world, to the USA, Iceland, India and Nepal, China, Australasia and the Pacific, north Africa and much of Europe. *Blue Horizons* is his second book.

David Paterson was born in Perth, and educated at Golspie High School and Edinburgh University. He worked for several years in industry and local government before turning full-time to photography in 1971. He has since worked for many leading advertising agencies, design groups and book and magazine publishers around the world. He has published a number of books on subjects ranging from the Himalayas to English landscape, and in 1990 founded Peak Publishing, dedicated to the production of high-quality books of his own and other photographers' work. Photography has also taken him to many countries, though in his personal work he now concentrates on the Scottish Highlands and the Nepal Himalaya, with nine visits to the latter since 1979. He is married to Mayumi, who is Japanese, and they have an18-year-old son, Sean.

Iain Roy grew up in East Lothian where he formed his lifelong attachment to the great outdoors. He was educated at George Heriot's School, Edinburgh, and graduated from Edinburgh University and the College of Art with an MA in Fine Art. He moved south to begin his career in 1967, first teaching history of art at Stourbridge College of Art and then to Brighton where he is now principal lecturer in photography. He has travelled widely and throughout the '80s and '90s has made many summer trips to Greenland. The British North East Greenland Project of which he and his wife, Fiona, are members was formed in 1990. This small group is dedicated to reaching remote corners of the fjord region of north-east Greenland. He hopes to publish a major study of this region in the near future. In 1992 he was the author of *Photographers' Britain: Sussex* (Alan Sutton Publishing) based on the landscape near his home in Brighton.

Photographic credits:
M. McQueen: front cover, pages 3-5, 9, 11-13, 23-25, 47-49, 56, 63, 65-67, 72-79, 96-101, 105-107, 109-123, 128, 130, 131, 136, 138, 142
D.Paterson: rear cover, pages 6, 14-22, 26, 27, 45, 50-55, 57-61, 69, 70, 83, 87, 89-95, 102-104, 125, 127, 129, 132-135, 137, 139-141, 143
I. Roy: pages 29, 30, 32-43, 68, 80-82 & 84-85

Further information on Peak Publishing can be found on the internet at www.wildcountry.uk.com